Movie Mutts

Hollywood Goes to the Dogs

MOVIE MUTTS

HOLLYWOOD
GOES TO THE DOGS

by
Stephen M. Silverman
with
COCO
the Dog

HARRY N. ABRAMS, INC., PUBLISHERS

To Sarah Anne Silverman and Harrison David Silverman, with lots of love from both authors

About the Author

Coco, a chocolate-colored retriever mix, was born on February 27, 1997, and rescued from the Manhattan branch of the ASPCA on July 9, 1998. She lives in New York's Financial District with the writer Stephen M. Silverman, whose several books include *Funny Ladies: 100 Years of Great Comediennes* and the biographies of the film directors David Lean and Stanley Donen.

Editor: Harriet Whelchel

Designer: Carol Robson

Back-cover art: Joe Zeff

Library of Congress Cataloging-in-Publication-Data

Silverman, Stephen M.
    Movie Mutts : Hollywood goes to the dogs / by Stephen M. Silverman with Coco.
      p. cm.
    Includes index.
    ISBN 0–8109–4394–8
      1. Dogs in motion pictures. I. Title.

    PN1995.9.A5 S56 2001
    791.43'6629772–dc21

                         00–052198

Published in 2001 by Harry N. Abrams, Incorporated, New York
All rights reserved. No part of the contents of this book may be reproduced without the written permission of the publisher

Printed and bound in Hong Kong

ABRAMS
Harry N. Abrams, Inc.
100 Fifth Avenue
New York, N.Y. 10011
www.abramsbooks.com

On the cover: Lassie and a movie camera, two of Hollywood's more enduring symbols

Endpapers: M-G-M's Flash posing with two starlets

Page 2: The title character in *My Dog Skip*, 2000, a big wheel by any measure

CONTENTS

FOREWORD: SAY HELLO TO COCO

AND MEAN DON'T CHANEL

By Rex Rover,
syndicated entertainment columnist

I've interviewed some real bitches in my time, but never have I actually encountered the genuine article. Welcome to the inevitable, I suppose. And none of those cracks about my career going to the dogs. But enough with the humor, and more about me.

I am here to introduce you to a dog named Coco, a svelte, chocolate-colored retriever mix of a typically Hollywood indeterminate age who shares her February 27 birthday with Elizabeth Taylor. (They also share the same long Maybelline eyelashes.) Well, I thought Ava Gardner came from a dirt-poor background, but that's nothing compared to Coco's. At least Ava came from North Carolina, which has some cachet. (It's Down South.) But Coco? From Staten Island. For those of you not as lucky as I to live in Manhattan, that's one of the outer boroughs. A very outer borough. Billy Bob Thornton wouldn't be caught dead there. Maybe.

But as I was saying, Coco was rescued off that outré outpost by the ASPCA—here the details get very *Tobacco Road*—after her initial owner chased after her with a pitchfork. She was then taken to the exclusive Upper East Side of Manhattan, where she was cared for in the animal shelter until she was adopted . . . and returned. The reason was because the adopter, a young woman, had given Coco to her boyfriend, an actor who, it turned out, didn't want a dog. (Competition, no doubt.) Finally, at the age of fifteen months, Coco was rescued by her

Coco at her manual typewriter, though she prefers to dictate.

current human, and, despite some occasionally heated arguments over who gets the bed, theirs appears to be a match made in M-G-M–style heaven.

So much for her checkered past. And *who* is Coco, you ask. (Well, I did.) She's never been in Liz Smith's column, so you're probably wondering what *I'm* doing writing about her. I just couldn't resist. She's a real movie hound. She sits in front of a large-screen television with all the wide-eyed wonderment of a young Margaret O'Brien and catches movies in the rather quaint penthouse she occupies in trendy Lower Manhattan. She doesn't exactly *watch* these movies, but she listens to the sounds they make and then responds doggedly (pun intended). A phone ringing on the sound-track of a DVD can literally send her into tailspins. And she'll always sit up for James Earl Jones's voice, especially when the bass is turned on full blast. But what really sends her into spasms of ecstasy is when she hears the newborn puppy yelping early into Walt Disney's *Lady and the Tramp.* No sooner does little Lady come burbling across the soundtrack than Coco scampers to the rear of the TV, in search of where the noise is coming from.

Such a reaction has resulted in this book, which, I have discovered, was the brainchild of Coco's agent. (The human with whom Coco resides, a writer, had spent four and a half years working on the biography of a particularly grumpy movie director, an experience that made him vow never to write about Hollywood again.) The agent, herself an animal fancier, not only convinced Coco's human *but also an actual publisher* that there are *a lot* of people out there who are curious about dogs in the movies. (She'll be in the proverbial doghouse if that proves not to be so, especially after the Great Dane–size advance Coco reputedly received.)

I've been made privy to Coco's manuscript. I would have done a better job, but I was busy alphabetizing my CDs. And while it's a pretty solid little book, I must say that some of Coco's decisions leave *me* howling at the moon. I mean, what in the world was she thinking when she didn't include Toto and Asta in her roster of All Stars? Has Coco got something against dogs with four-letter names? I mean, cripes, Toto starred with JUDY. That should make the little guy All Star enough. I just don't buy Coco's argument that Toto wasn't the star of the picture, or that he didn't go on to make a name for himself in other movies. And Asta? Coco supposedly did some market research and discovered that the name is no longer familiar to modern audiences. Tsk to modern audiences, I say. And as for market research: did James Cameron stoop to market research in deciding whether or not to sink the *Titanic*?

Right: **Coco in disguise, to thwart autograph-seekers.** *Below:* **Asta, of M-G-M's** ***The Thin Man*** **series, awaits her trainer's cues as a photographer just happens to be on hand.**

Now, just to keep you on the straight and narrow, this is a book about dogs of the movies—Rin Tin Tin, Lassie, and other big-name barkers of the silver screen. No little TV parvenu pooches here. Nor is this about movie dogs—or turkeys, if you prefer—such abominations as *Ishtar, Battlefield Earth,* or *The Mirror Has Two Faces.*

Joyfully, this is strictly about those four-legged, four-star friends who supplied their own fur coats to the flickers . . . with one exception. Inside the book you'll find a shot of Clark Gable with his personal pet. But then, we *are* talking about the King of Hollywood. Clark, I mean.

Blissful browsing,
you bookish Bowsers,

Dogs in the Movies:
The More, The Terrier

Then, as now, it was the public that created stars. Early moviegoers, thwarted by the business-minded studio bosses' decree that an anonymous movie actor was also a bargain-salaried actor, demanded to know who that was they were watching. Thus, in 1910, Hollywood's first movie star was born: Florence Lawrence, previously known simply (and solely) as the Biograph Girl, until producer Carl Laemmle bought out her Biograph contract and presented Lawrence under his own aegis—and under her own name. Her far-reaching celebrity quickly paved the way for the subsequent rise of other performers, including Charlie Chaplin, Douglas Fairbanks, and Mary Pickford, whose prodigious stature and influence would soon exceed that of Lawrence's.

Talkies may have torpedoed some screen careers but not that of Rin Tin Tin, whose smooth transition to sound was publicized by this 1929 studio still. That's owner-trainer Lee Duncan standing on two legs (to the left).

Impressive as her accomplishment may be, Lawrence's ascent on American shores came a good half decade after another name had already caused a sensation in England—in a stage-bound, six-minute movie about a baby who is kidnapped from under the nose of her nanny. The baby was not the star, but, rather, her rescuer: a collie mix named Rover. The 1905 motion picture *Rescued by Rover,* directed by Lewis Fitzhamon and produced by British cinema trailblazer Cecil Hepworth (who cast his own family in the endeavor), was essentially a chase film, in which the camera tracked Rover from the time of the infant's abduction by gypsies to the dog's discovering the hideaway and then fetching the father to bring about a tearful reunion with his daughter.

Good as Rover was, he was not the first dog to reveal his noble character on screen. In France, home to much of the moviemaking development (simultaneous to Thomas Edison's invention of the Kinetoscope in New Jersey), the inaugural program of the brothers Auguste and Louis Lumière's hand-cranked contraption, the Cinématographe, was the 1895 *Workers Leaving the Lumière Factory.* The historic strip of film was really nothing more than the stationary camera's capturing of a parade of women employees filing out of the Lumière headquarters in Lyons. Dutifully waiting for them outside the factory gates as the workday ended: a loyal dog.

Back on American shores, conflicting reports exist as to who can lay claim to being the first canine star. In 1910, Vitagraph (a competitor to Biograph) spotlighted Jean, the Vitagraph Dog, a border collie mix belonging to an actor-writer at the studio, Laurence Trimble. Trimble not only served as Jean's guardian, ensuring that the pooch did precisely what was required for the camera, but he also ended up directing an entire series of movies

starring Jean and the actress Florence Turner, better known as the Vitagraph Girl (an ostensible rival to Biograph Girl Florence Lawrence, right down to the duplication of the first name). Popular as Jean may have been in the years just prior to World War I, today he remains but a footnote in the annals of Hollywood. Trimble, meanwhile, went on to make a kind of name for himself thanks to his association with another dog altogether, a heroic German shepherd whose screen name was Strongheart. Their celebrated collaboration began in the early 1920s, some ten years after the debut of Jean.

Hollywood historians Richard Griffith and Arthur Mayer, in a mid-twentieth-century overview of the picture business, credited Ben, the Mack Sennett dog, as being the first nonhuman movie star. Yet little record of Ben exists. Certainly there remains footage of Teddy, or

America's first four-legged star was Jean, the Vitagraph Dog, whose vibrant yet short-lived career began in 1910.

"Keystone Teddy," as leading lady Gloria Swanson called him— Keystone being the name of producer Sennett's studio, at which the large Lab mix made a good number of appearances as a comic cohort. (Sennett specialized in slapstick comedy.) In 1917, Teddy costarred with Swanson and Wallace Beery in Keystone's *Teddy at the Throttle.*

The young Gloria Swanson is pulled from peril by the titular leading man of *Teddy at the Throttle* (1917), from slapstick comedy king **Mack Sennett.**

"At the end of the picture," Swanson recalled in her 1980 memoir, *Swanson on Swanson,* "the villain [Beery] ties the sweet young heroine [Swanson] to the railroad tracks, but before the train can run over her, her boyfriend's marvelous dog, Teddy, alerts the engineer and saves the day." (That old damsel-in-distress trick dates back to 1914, at least, with the Pathé serial *The Perils of Pauline,* starring the action performer Pearl White. But leave it to Sennett to cast a dog in the role of romantic hero.)

One notable Sennett star with whom Teddy appears not to have shared screen time was Charlie Chaplin, who, starting in December of 1912, made some thirty-five films in his one-year tenure at Keystone. In 1915, for Essanay, Chaplin made *The Champion,* which contained an opening routine involving Chaplin's trademark Tramp character sharing his hot dog with a finicky bulldog. Three years later, having graduated from two-reelers to three and to his very own studio, Chaplin cast himself opposite a dog named Mut—called "Scraps, a thoroughbred mongrel" in the scenario—for what would be for Chaplin a watershed film, *A Dog's Life.*

"The story had an element of satire, paralleling the life of a dog with that of a tramp," Chaplin recalled for his 1964 *My Autobiography,* neglecting, as he does throughout his book, to credit his costar for *his* screen presence. (Mut timidly peers around a street corner to gaze upon a cop on the beat with a melancholy to match anything Chaplin himself could muster.) Juxtaposing the tramp's life with the dog's, Chaplin, apparently accepting Scraps as his alter ego, "was beginning to think of comedy in a structural sense, and to become conscious of its architectural form," the filmmaker said. "Each sequence implied the next sequence, all of them relating to the whole."

The first bit of action involved "rescuing a dog from a fight with other dogs." In this, Chaplin borrows a familiar routine of Keystone Teddy's—that of biting the villain's coattail—but comically improves upon it, thanks in large part to the antics of the dog. Talk about earning one's chops: While the Little Tramp safely nestles Scraps in his arms, a bigger (and even scrappier) dog attaches itself to the back of Charlie's garment. Instead of being stopped dead in his tracks, as was generally meant to happen whenever Teddy latched onto someone, Chaplin executes a balletic twirl that lifts his attacker off the ground and sends him spinning.

"The next sequence was rescuing a girl in a dance hall who was also leading 'a dog's life,'" said Chaplin. "There were many other sequences, all of which followed in a logical concatenation of events." All concludes logically, as well. The Little Tramp and the

Mut (right), the costar of Charlie Chaplin's *A Dog's Life* (1918), won the role after tens of other aspirants failed their auditions.

dance-hall girl end up happily married, sharing their home with Scraps and the brood of offspring he has sired. Fade out. Only it wasn't simply the puppy population that was on the rise, so was Chaplin's stock; the pioneer French film critic Louis Delluc, whose 1921 book-length study of Chaplin, *Charlot,* was the first serious appreciation of the writer-director-producer-star, declared *A Dog's Life* "the first complete work of art the cinema has. It is classical. It *exists.*"

On a more temporal level, Chaplin biographer David Robinson has revealed that Mut had not occupied the inside track as far as casting was concerned. In December of 1916, a full year before *A Dog's Life* commenced production, the studio took out newspaper ads declaring "Chaplin Wants a Dog with Lots of Comedy Sense." Hardly bashful when it came to publicity, the filmmaker told reporters that his first applicant was a dachshund, although, Chaplin was to concede, "The long snaky piece of hose got on my nerves. I bought him from a fat man named Ehrmentraut, and when Sausages went back to his master I made no kick." Next came a Pomeranian brought to the studio by Chaplin's leading lady, Edna Purviance, "who had him clipped where he ought to have worn hair and left him with whiskers where he didn't need them." The tonsorial victim was quickly swapped for a poodle, though the poor creature had no better luck than Purviance's Pomeranian. Sniffed Chaplin: "That moon-eyed snuffling little beast lasted two days."

A Boston bull terrier was screen-tested, followed by a pedigreed English bulldog who went by the name of Bandy. Still no go. Then a lightbulb went off above Chaplin's head. "What I really want is a mongrel dog," he realized. "These studio beasts are too well kept." Chaplin claimed to be combing the back alleys of Hollywood in search of a dog hungry enough to respond to the offering of a bone—a sure sign that the animal would take direction. Twenty-one strays from the Los Angeles pound were summarily delivered to the Chaplin Studios, though about nine of them had to be sent back when neighbors complained about the noise factor.

Apparently, Mut was one of the twelve who remained behind, and, with him in the title role, *A Dog's Life* rolled before the cameras from January 15 to April 9 of 1918. As David Robinson recounted in his 1985 *Chaplin: His Life and Art,* "The studio petty cash accounts show entries for dogs' meat starting from the second week of production and continuing until the end of shooting." Furthermore, Robinson confirmed, after filming was completed, Mut took up permanent residence at the studio "and remained on staff until his untimely death."

Not that Mut was ever known to have made another movie.

Beginning in 1921, Vitagraph's Strongheart, né Etzel von Oeringen, was the screen's first and foremost German shepherd, paving the way for M-G-M's Flash and the most successful dog of his kind (or of any kind), Warner Bros.'s Rin Tin Tin.

The first canine screen star of significant consequence was Vitagraph's Strongheart, who rose to prominence at the dawn of the twenties. The shepherd's kennel name in his native Germany was Etzel von Oeringen, and his father, Nores von der Kriminal Politzei, was perennially unchallenged at dog shows until little Etzel came along and claimed his titles. Perhaps "little" is a misnomer: At the age of three, in 1920, when he was discovered for the movies and renamed Strongheart, Etzel's weight hovered somewhere between 115 and 125 pounds.

Strongheart was imported to America by Laurence Trimble, who, since his directing success with Jean, the Vitagraph Dog, had been performing in English music halls with his lifelong friend, Florence Turner (the Vitagraph Girl). Along with the writer Jane Murfin, author of *Lilac Time,* Trimble was convinced that Strongheart should be taken to Hollywood for the specific purpose of becoming a star. The move was unprecedented given that, while other four-legged performers may have previously appeared on screen, they had always been confined to supporting roles.

But what the two movie people discovered was that Etzel/Strongheart's training in his native land had been so militaristic that it had knocked out of him any sense of playfulness or spontaneity—distinctive traits that Trimble and Murfin were hoping would register with moviegoers. Painstakingly, over several months, the director sought to reeducate his charge. "One of his basic rules is always to permit an animal to 'save face,'" recalled J. Allen Boone, who had helped to chronicle the Strongheart saga. "Never embarrass it, no matter what the animal may have done or neglected to do."

The stories of Trimble's deregimenting Strongheart play up a basic, mutually appreciative relationship between man and beast. Trimble, said Boone, devised "innumerable simple, almost childlike methods for winning first the interest, then the respect, then the trust" of the animal. From there, Trimble persuaded Strongheart to turn to him instinctively whenever the dog felt confused. As Boone explained in a 1954 discourse (long after Strongheart had met his maker, but, ironically, the same year Trimble had died):

> [Trimble] knows that every animal wants to think well of itself, wants to be understood, wants to be appreciated, and wants to find and be its best self. But he also knows how sensitive animals are to the mental atmosphere around them, and how arresting to their growth it is to hurt their feelings, to ridicule them, to nag at them, to laugh at them, to confuse them, to look upon them with contempt, or to correct them in the wrong way. . . .
>
> "When you are with an animal," Trimble once told me, "never be surprised when he does what you ask, even when you ask the first time. Always expect the impossible to happen."

By 1921, the impossible *did* happen: Strongheart was an irrefutable star, receiving stacks of fan mail and attracting as large a throng of reporters to greet him at New York's Grand Central Station as did any Vitagraph player. His first movie, directed by Trimble and scripted by Murfin (as were all his vehicles), was

The Silent Call, an outdoor adventure whose success rested largely upon the novelty of there being a dog in the leading role. Strongheart, Trimble, and Murfin followed with *Brawn of the North* (1922), *The Love Master* (1924), and the first of several screen adaptations of Jack London's *White Fang* (1925), in which Strongheart took on the role of a wolf. Because of the movies' success, hypothesized a highly biased J. Allen Boone, "Other German shepherd dogs were brought from Germany, new 'sensational dog finds' were made in this country, and all hurried to Hollywood as starring material. But the incomparable Strongheart towered above them all in looks, character, accomplishments, and audience appeal."

While Boone could have been referring to Flash, the M-G-M shepherd, his dagger was more clearly pointed at the most famous movie German shepherd of all time, Rin Tin Tin. The four-legged Warner Bros. star so often kept that financially beleaguered studio from going under during its checkered early career (until such time in 1927 when Al Jolson opened his mouth and words came out in Warner's *The Jazz Singer)* that Rinty's potent box-office draw caused appreciative theater exhibitors to refer to him as "the mortgage-lifter."

As for his own efforts during his enviable screen career, Rinty earned some five million dollars—and this was back in the days before taxes.

As with any Hollywood star, discrepancies exist as to the actual age of Rin Tin Tin. Some reports say that he was born in 1916—his 1932 obituaries stated he was sixteen at the time of his death—while another birth date, that of September 13, 1918, seems more convincing, given that, shortly after the end of World War I, Rinty's American-soldier owner brought him to Hollywood.

Legend holds (and it might as well keep holding) that Rinty was one of six puppies born to a near-starving German shepherd near an airfield in Fleury, France, in a trench that had been dug and then abandoned by some of Kaiser Wilhelm's finest. Captain (some accounts rank him as sergeant) Leland Duncan, known as Lee, a twenty-nine-year-old noncommissioned American Air Corps pilot, stumbled upon the shell-shocked dogs and took them back to the U.S. military base, where they were bathed and fed and, once old enough to be weaned from their mother, dispersed among the soldiers for safekeeping. Duncan kept two for himself and named them Rin Tin Tin and Nanette, after two mythic French lovers who, during World War I, were reputedly the sole survivors of a German bombing attack on a railway station that claimed the lives of forty others.

Duncan's Nanette died of pneumonia only three days after reaching America, but Rin Tin Tin survived. And how. Duncan enrolled him in a dog show, but Rinty performed so clumsily that his owner undertook for him a rigorous training program, beginning with holding a finger to the dog's forehead and then praising Rinty when he would sit—which he did, sometimes for as long as three minutes, even with Duncan out of sight. Using soft objects, Duncan next taught Rinty how to fetch, generally in a long, indoor hallway, so as not to disturb Rinty's concentration with any outside influences.

Possibly, Duncan thought, his companion might make a name for himself in vaudeville, but, instead, they chose a path to the movies. Rinty's first appearance was in 1922's *The Man from Hell's River,* which was enough to get him noticed by studio head of production Jack Warner. He then enlisted favored director Mal St. Clair to develop an entire series of films to star this heroic-looking dog. St. Clair, in turn, dragged in a newcomer to help with the project, an aspiring screenwriter he knew from the Los Angeles Athletic Club. The writer's name was Darryl F. Zanuck, and within the next dozen years the young Nebraska native would rise to prominence in Hollywood and end up leading his own studio, Twentieth Century Fox. But first there was his collaboration with Rinty.

As *The New York Times* said of Rinty's second movie (and the first in which he starred), 1923's *Where the North Begins,* the leading man may have possessed "splendid eyes and ears," but his acting ability left something to be desired. "This dog engages in a pantomimic struggle that is not always impressive, at least not as realistic as the work of Strongheart," said the *Times.* "But in one sequence when he is shown a piece of the villain's trousers, he is made to appear in a most vicious mood."

During pre-production, Zanuck and St. Clair would act out their scenarios for Warner in his office, with Zanuck playing the part of the dog. That meant jumping onto Warner's desk. (Later, Zanuck would chase secretaries around his own desk, causing many women to liken him to a wolf.) Most of the storylines for the numerous features and serials in which Rinty starred—until 1931, when Rin Tin Tin, Jr., who had been introduced in 1927's *Hills of Kentucky,* grabbed the elder Rinty's baton and ran with it—focused on the animal's slavish devotion to his masters. "Rin Tin Tin could do anything," Zanuck told one of his biographers, Mel Gussow. "Actually, there were about five or six Rin Tin Tins at one time— one for long shots, one for close-ups, one to play gentle parts, one to fight. Another could jump and do terrific stunts. Another had marvelous eyes." At the height of his fame, Rinty received some 2,000 fan letters a week—which, as one wag pointed out, was only 286 a week in dog years. He was also one star in Hollywood who did not lose sleep over the transition to sound.

In 1932, at the age of fourteen, or sixteen, Rinty even died a star's death—in the arms of his Beverly Hills neighbor, M-G-M's blond bombshell Jean Harlow. She reportedly saw him collapse on Duncan's lawn next door and ran to his side. Rinty was shipped to France for burial, and he remains there to this day, in the Cimetière des Chiens et Autres Animaux Exotiques, in the Parisian suburb of Asnières. His tombstone of black onyx carries the gold-leafed inscription STAR OF THE CINEMA.

Meanwhile, the various Rintys who appeared on the 1950s television program *The Adventures of Rin-Tin-Tin* (which inexplicably added hyphens to the star's name) are eternally sleeping somewhere on the estate that once belonged to Lee Duncan.

William Powell and Myrna Loy regard man's best friend, Asta, who costarred with them in M-G-M's six-film *The Thin Man* series (1934–47). The popular wire-haired fox terrier, meanwhile, contemplates a dog's best friend.

"Several wire-haired terriers played our scene-stealing pet over the years," Loy recalled in her 1987 memoir, *Myrna Loy: Being and Becoming,* "but we weren't allowed to make friends with any of them. The trainer feared it would break the dogs' concentration." Furthermore, revealed Loy, the very first Asta, whose real name was Skippy, "bit me once, so our relationship was hardly idyllic."

As for how film critics reacted to dogs in movies, one need only cite James Agee. As he mused in his October 8, 1943, column for *The Nation:*

> *Lassie Come Home* is a dog story which I had hardly expected to enjoy, and cannot be sure who will and who won't. I did, though. Those who made it seem to have had a pretty fair sense of the square naïveté which most good stories for children have, or affect; they also manipulate some surprisingly acute emotions out of the head dog. Whether from private remembrance or from the show, I got several reverberations of that strangely pure, half-magical tone which certain books, regardless of their other qualities, have for many children.

Take that, Harry Potter. M-G-M's Technicolor version of *Lassie Come Home* was based on a 1938 short story that originally appeared in *The Saturday Evening Post* before it was expanded into a popular novella the following year. Its author, Eric Knight, a former newspaper reporter and film critic, had been born in Yorkshire, England, but raised in the United States, on whose behalf he had served during World War I. During World War II, he helped write the documentary series *Why We Fight* with the director Frank Capra. In Capra's autobiography, *The Name Above the Title,* the filmmaker fondly recalled Knight as "a Yorkshireman whose unruly shock of dark red hair seemed as full of mischief as his sharp, ferret-like eyes," and expressed profound grief upon hearing the news, on January 14, 1943, that Knight's plane had been shot down en route to Cairo, where he was to have opened a new Armed Forces Radio Station. Capra had heard that the aircraft carrying Knight was misidentified over the Caribbean by a U-boat that thought the plane had a Casablanca-bound President Roosevelt on board.

Knight had modeled Lassie after his own dog, Toots, "the most warm, the most loyal, the most loving, devoted dog," Knight's widow, Jere, once proclaimed. In the story, and the remarkably faithful (if, by today's standards, plodding) film adaptation, Knight

To get Lassie to lick Roddy McDowall in *Lassie Come Home* (1943), studio prop men applied ice cream to the child actor's face.

presented Lassie as a steadfast collie who surmounts tortuous obstacles in a yearlong trek from Scotland to Yorkshire, England, back to the poor family—and to the son, Joe—that had been forced, out of financial necessity, to sell her to a wealthy duke.

Three hundred aspirants—or more than one thousand, depending upon which M-G-M press release one cares to believe—auditioned for the role of Lassie, who ended up being played by a male collie named Pal. (Males, while considered less intelligent, and less nervous, than their female counterparts, sport fuller manes and are said to photograph better.) "They couldn't get a bitch for the part that looked right," Knight wrote to his wife during production, "so he's a female impersonator— and thank God he's got a long coat that covers his manhood."

Pal was not a classically handsome example of his breed. He stood smaller than a standard collie—just as human movie stars tend to be shorter than the average person—and lacked the long, narrow nose associated with most of his kind. On the rise of his nose he sported an atypical narrow white blaze that opened into a perfectly formed oval on his forehead; a beautiful marking, to be sure, but enough to have disqualified him from winning a blue ribbon in a show.

On the other hand, few disputed Pal's intelligence, or the diligence of his owner-trainers, Frank and Rudd Weatherwax. The brothers—who grew up on the California ranch of their father, a one-time deputy U.S. Marshall (in Texas), Walter "Smiley" Weatherwax—had done some acting, but they hit their stride training animals for the studios, a craft they had undertaken by accident in the early 1920s, after a little fox terrier they named Wiggles had simply shown up at their door. When Rudd Weatherwax was cast as an extra, at the age of fourteen, to play a messenger in a movie scene, he brought along his foundling, who clutched the telegram in his mouth. (Wiggles subsequently enjoyed a two-year career.)

Lassie, or, rather, Pal, had come to Rudd Weatherwax as a noisy, uncontrollable, yet considerably bright eight-month-old. His owner had deposited the dog at the brothers' training school, but, as Weatherwax recounted in his 1971 book, *The Lassie Method,*

Lassie inspired even more spin-offs than *Star Wars.* In *Son of Lassie* (1945, two years after the superior original) mother and son—actually played by two male collies—assisted the British in the fight against the Nazis.

"When I called the man to pick up Pal, he didn't want him any longer and asked if I would take the collie in lieu of the seventy-dollar training bill." A wise investment, to be sure, though Lassie's bankbook had yet to rival that of Rin Tin Tin's (at least not until later television and product-merchandising incarnations). M-G-M may have made millions off of Lassie, but Weatherwax earned only a reported $264,000 from the dog's association with the studio.

(On the other hand, in the early 1950s, when the shortsighted M-G-M still owed him $40,000, Weatherwax proposed that the studio simply let him have Lassie outright in exchange for the sum, and they called it a deal.) Knight's estate fared much worse, because he had been paid a flat fee by M-G-M for his story. He received no future royalties, either, having sold off all ancillary rights at the time of his original contract.

The success of the first Lassie movie spawned six feature-length sequels, produced through 1951, in which four different descendants of the original Pal starred. A national radio show debuted on ABC in 1947—Pal did the barking on the show while all other canine-associated noises, from panting to whimpering, were supplied by a human actor. (Real-life dogs who tuned in presumably noticed the difference.) And a long-running television series, which scrapped all previous storylines from the movies and placed Lassie in a rural family setting, debuted on CBS in 1954.

In the 1970s, Lassie—in the form of a sixth-generation descendant of Pal—returned to the large screen in *The Magic of Lassie,* starring James Stewart and Alice Faye, who, like their canine costar, had seen better days. Still, the picture clicked with young audiences, and in New York, where it played Radio City Music Hall, Lassie herself appeared on the great stage—when she wasn't taking it easy in her $380-a-night suite at the Plaza Hotel. And Chaplin questioned a dog's life?

The 1930s and 1940s were a Golden Age not only for the Hollywood studios, but also for the dog stars and their trainers. Frank and Rudd Weatherwax, together with the trainer Henry East, with whom they had been associated in 1923, wrangled Asta for the screen, as well as the mutt Daisy in the *Blondie* series and the titular big yellow dog of *Old Yeller.* Yet another Weatherwax brother, Jack, took a job with the trainer Carl Spitz and handled a familiar-looking cairn terrier named Terry, better known as Toto in *The Wizard of Oz.* So high-profile was Spitz that a photograph in Aljean Harmetz's definitive behind-the-scenes movie book, *The Making of*

Clark Gable and Loretta Young starred in the 1935 screen version of Jack London's 1903 novel *The Call of the Wild*, which had originally been serialized in *The Saturday Evening Post*. Its action concerned a St. Bernard named Buck, "a tidewater dog, strong of muscle and with warm, long hair," as described by London.

"*The Wizard of Oz*," shows the trainer on a 1940 "Hollywood Motion Picture Dog Preview" public appearance tour. With him are Promise, the pointer from *The Biscuit Eater;* Buck, the St. Bernard from *The Call of the Wild;* Terry (aka Toto); Prince, the Great Dane from *Wuthering Heights;* Mr. Binkie, the Scottie from *The Light That Failed;* and Musty, the mastiff from *Dangerous Days.* Harmetz reported the value of the six dogs to be $120,000, in 1940 dollars. Alas, the gravy train ended in the 1950s when television eroded the power of the movie companies and sent many of the dogs scurrying to the small screen.

As an increasingly diverse Hollywood entered the twenty-first century, stars of the *Canis* genus had become as equally accomplished as their *Homo sapien* counterparts. And while John Travolta had proved by the late 1970s that a television actor could successfully sustain the leap from the small screen to the big, as would Bruce Willis a decade later, several other human actors—Shelly Long, David Caruso, nearly the entire cast of *Friends*—found it rougher going.

Such was hardly the case with a miniature mutt of cocker, poodle, and schnauzer heritage named Higgins, who originally had been rescued at the Burbank Animal Shelter by the trainer Frank Inn, a former apprentice with Rudd Weatherwax. His Higgins ended up costarring as the sneezy little pet who inhabited the downstairs of Hooterville's Shady Rest Hotel on the 1963–70 CBS situation comedy *Petticoat Junction.* A master of the double take, Higgins was semiretired when an aspiring Dallas-based filmmaker named Joe Camp approached Inn with his idea to produce a low-budget, homespun, family film about a dog who assists in the recovery of two kidnapped children—essentially a plot no more sophisticated than that found in *Rescued by Rover.* The movie, taking its title from the name of the lead character, would be called *Benji.*

Inn's reaction? "You don't want Higgins. He's thirteen or fourteen years old." Camp would not be deterred, however, and in 1974 Higgins was seen slogging his way through his first movie caper, which may have set critics' teeth on edge but which made several millions of dollars for its maker. Sequels followed, starring a Higgins facsimile (albeit slimmer), and Benji, like Rin Tin Tin and Lassie before him, assumed his place amid the Hollywood supernovas.

Far more recently, a Jack Russell terrier named Moose, seemingly forever stereotyped as the frisky Eddie on the television sitcom *Frasier,* displayed his range when he starred in *My Dog Skip,* based on Willie Morris's memoir of growing up in a small Mississippi town during World War II. Whereas on television Moose comes across as little more than a mischievous pup whose high hand dependably triggers Frasier Crane's slow burn, on the big screen

Even before John Travolta successfully made the leap from small screen to large in the 1970s, Benji—actually, a miniature scene-stealer of mixed heritage named Higgins—graduated from character actor on television's *Petticoat Junction* to starring in a successful movie series all his own.

My Dog Skip (2000) starred two TV favorites, *Malcolm in the Middle*'s Frankie Muniz and *Frasier*'s Eddie (real name: Moose), though, in fact, several "Skips," including an automated robot version, were used throughout the picture. Here, the two protagonists awake after a scary night in a cemetery.

he elicits both laughter and sympathy without stooping to the cheap, saccharine tricks that have plagued so many of his predecessors. All the more impressive is that in Morris's book, Skip wasn't a Jack Russell at all, but a purebred, smooth-haired English fox terrier. Nevertheless, once Moose got through enchanting audiences as Skip, it was impossible to envision the character as anything *but* a Jack Russell.

Not that such a theatrical transmogrification came easily, as evidenced by the rules by which, during production, the rest of the cast was forced to abide:

> Don't touch the dog, don't speak to the dog, don't look the dog in the eye, and don't eat in front of the dog.

Talk about star power.

Ah yes, but one wonders, will Moose have staying power? That is something only the movie dogs—or, rather, gods—can answer.

Doggedly Determined: Action Stars

Ever faithful Rin Tin Tin, in *Jaws of Steel* (1927), costarring with Mary Lousie Miller. The actor Jason Robards, Sr., played her father in the silent screenplay.

If Rin Tin Tin were alive and in movies today, he'd be Harrison Ford. Ample muscles, only not *too* many. Strong, silent type, but says what he has to. And just the right amount of mileage on him. He could have pawed me any time.

—Coco

Clark Gable as Jack Thornton, who wins the dog Buck in a card game before both man and beast head for the Yukon in 1935's *The Call of the Wild*, based on the Jack London tale.

1936's *White Fang*, also from the pen of Jack London, involved a gold mine, a murder, and a faithful wolf-dog—successful elements, obviously, because the movie was remade at least three other times.

1946's *Courage of Lassie* marked the third entry in the M-G-M franchise and starred the beloved collie as a maladjusted soldier home from World War II (where she still managed to perform heroics, as shown here).

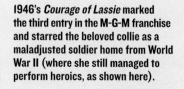

Kevin Corcoran
splashes about as Arliss
Coates in Walt Disney's 1957
Christmas release, *Old Yeller*,
from the Fred Gipson novel about a
lop-eared dog in the 1860s who walks into
a lonely Western family's life and changes it
for the better (until the elder son is forced to kill
the rabid pet). The film could be viewed today as
being politically incorrect, what with the gunplay of
Arliss and his elder brother, Travis (Tommy Kirk),
and the way in which animals are annihilated.

Old Yeller is a four-hankie tearjerker as far as humans are concerned, but I simply prefer to take the entire box of Kleenex, bite into it, shake it so that the cardboard ends become undone, then really go to town in the living room. It's funny how well Kleenex flies all on its own. Do this, and I promise: It's a great way to get your human to stop crying over *Old Yeller*.

—Coco

Trained dogs have been performing for the public ever since the days of the ancient Roman circuses. Even then, there were those who complained that these animals should be allowed to run free. As for my own position on the matter, I prefer to quote the Swedish author August Strindberg (1849–1912): "I loathe people who keep dogs. They are the cowards who haven't got the guts to bite people themselves."

—Coco

Lassie in one of her many incarnations, this time in
1994's *Lassie,* in which she teaches a city family the
ways of farm life.

Right: Disney remade its 1963 *The Incredible Journey*—about three pets separated from their family: a naïve puppy, a wise old dog, and a snooty cat—as 1993's *Homeward Bound: The Incredible Journey,* with the voices of the animals supplied by Michael J. Fox, Don Ameche, and Sally Field.

The fight for survival among the husky sled team in *Antarctica* (1983) made for a box-office hit in the film's native Japan, but not in America, where, despite a mesmerizing musical score by Vangelis, the narrative lost something in the translation.

No Disney film seems complete without an attack by a bear, be it *Old Yeller* or (here) *Homeward Bound: The Incredible Journey.*

Ethan Hawke starred in the 1991 version of the Jack London perennial, *White Fang,* which proved effective enough to warrant a sequel, 1994's *White Fang 2: The Myth of the White Wolf.* That one bites.

Another Japanese import, 1986's captivating *Milo and Otis,* followed the travails of a pug (Otis) and a cat who, after growing up together on a farm, become separated before embarking upon a search for one another.

Producer Steven Spielberg tried his hand at an animated Jack London-ish tale with 1995's, *Balto,* about a heroic half-wolf's fight to stop diphtheria from taking over Alaska in 1925.

Right: Buddy, a golden retriever better known as Air Bud in the 1997 basketball movie of the same name, lost a leg to diabetes soon after he starred in the movie and died before a second film was made. *Above:* 1998's *Air Bud: Golden Receiver* (both co-starred Kevin Zegers, to the left of Bud on the basketball court).

Howlers: Funny Dogs

"Keystone" Teddy comes between Bill Vernon and Gloria Swanson in 1917's *Teddy at the Throttle.*

Comedy headliner Louise Fazenda takes an obedient yet oversized Teddy for a ride in 1917 as they both get the once-over from producer Mack Sennett.

Buster Keaton is kept on the straight and narrow as he proposes to Ruth Dwyer in 1925's *Seven Chances* (which, in 1999, was remade as *The Bachelor* with Chris O'Donnell— only that time it was the movie that was the dog).

Teddy again, this time tugging on one end of Billy Armstrong while Louise Fazenda yanks on the other (*My Goodness*, 1920).

Polly Moran prepares for her *Honeymoon* (1928) while attended by Flash, M-G-M's answer to Rin Tin Tin.

Billy Bevan is stopped in his tracks by a tenacious pooch in 1928's *The Bicycle Flirt*.

Asked whether the dog tried to upstage him or Bing Crosby during the making of 1944's *The Road to Utopia*, Bob Hope replied: "You gotta be kiddin'."

Moviegoers traipsing in to see *Beethoven* and *Dr. Dolittle* should have been handed rolls of toilet paper along with their tickets. One bodily function joke is sufficient, but these movies waded in them . . . or waded in something. Not that I'm a prude. *There's Something About Mary* deserves two paws up, and, man, was it gross.

—Coco

Left: Charles Grodin played devoted dad and air-freshener merchant George Newton, whose domestic life is turned upside down by a loving though messy St. Bernard, in 1992's *Beethoven.* The following year, Grodin and the dog were back, as was a female companion for Beethoven, named Missy. Puppies, not surprisingly, figured heavily in the plot.

Below left: Eddie Murphy softened his comic image when he played a hard-nosed doctor who discovered he could converse with animals in 1998's *Dr. Dolittle,* to whom the dogs talked back, usually about matters relating to their butts.

Above: Christopher Guest skewered the snooty world of championship-dog breeding in his 2000 "mockumentary," *Best in Show.* Here the auteur, who played good ol' boy Harlan Pepper in the film, puckers up for his beloved bloodhound, Hubert, before the two of them face the judges.

Scamps: What? Me Have a Bath?

The most famous movie star to hate dogs was W. C. Fields. (Imagine saying, "Any man who hates dogs and children can't be all bad.") He claimed that dogs bit him from the time he was a boy with a paper route, and they never stopped. Maybe it was because we knew something his fellow man didn't. "Fields can give the impression to men that he is a highly respectable fellow," said a profile of the ornery comedian by Alva Johnston in *The New Yorker,* "but he cannot give that impression to dogs. Once a tramp, always a tramp, as far as dogs are concerned. Looking right through his fine clothes and synthetic dignity, they see the former hobo." Sorry, W. C.   —**Coco**

Charlie Chaplin and Mut, in the poignant comedy *A Dog's Life* (1918), in which it was frequently hard to determine whose lot was more doleful.

In 1923's *Peg O' My Heart,* Laurette Taylor plays a simple Irish girl named Peg, who is sent to live on the English estate of her wealthy grandfather, whose maid has misgivings about the behavior of Peg's pet—while Peg thinks nothing of it.

Bruce Bennett and a less-than-bashful Staffordshire bull terrier eye a food stand in *Flying Fists* (1937), a boxing drama in which the key fight is fixed, proving once again that only a dog can be trusted.

Top: Animator Don Bluth's only so-so *All Dogs Go to Heaven* (1989), featured the voices of Dom DeLuise, Burt Reynolds, and Loni Anderson, and brought to mind the James Thurber observation, "If I have any beliefs about immortality, it is that certain dogs I have known will go to heaven, and very, very few persons." **Right:** Jackie Cooper costarred with Robert Coogan in 1931's *Skippy*, based on a comic strip about two kids from the opposite sides of the track who try to scrape together three dollars to buy a dog license. **Opposite page:** In John Huston's much-maligned musical *Annie* (1982, with Aileen Quinn), also based on a comic strip, the bouncy song "Sandy" was added to the score to describe the plucky orphan's faithful, if flea-bitten, companion.

Above: Joe E. Brown played a horoscope-happy prize fighter in the 1937 slapstick comedy *When's Your Birthday?* Holding the dog, which looks like a well-balanced Libra, is Edgar Kennedy (better known for his slow burns over the antics of Laurel and Hardy), while Marian Marsh plays along.

Right: The prissy poodle Georgette (whose voice was supplied by Bette Milder) puts Tito (Cheech Marin) through his paces in Disney's *Oliver & Company,* a 1988 animated take on Charles Dickens's *Oliver Twist,* in which Fagin's boys are dogs and Oliver is a kitten.
Overleaf: Jack Nicholson owes a good deal of his 1997 Oscar for *As Good As It Gets* to Verdell, the Brussels griffon who charmed the Nicholson character (Melvin Udall) into lightening up. Verdell was actually Jill, whose owner-trainer Mathilde de Cagny has a fine eye for talent. Also in her acting stable were Clovis, the golden retriever who played Shadow in the 1993 film *Homeward Bound: The Incredible Journey,* and Moose, better known as Eddie on TV's *Frasier* and the star of *My Dog Skip.*

Playful Pups: Quick, Take Off the Leash

Director Zion Myers (1898–1948) occupies a distinctive niche in the Hollywood pantheon. A cousin of director Mark Sandrich, who guided such sublime Fred Astaire–Ginger Rogers vehicles as *Top Hat* and *The Gay Divorcée*, Myers's own filmography of the 1920s and 1930s, comprised exclusively of short subjects, reads like a dog lover's dream. Among his floppy-eared flicks (moments from which are captured here) are 1924's *A Dog's Pal*, 1930's *Who Killed Rover?* and *The Dogway Melody*, and three stellar productions from 1931: *The Two Barks Brothers* (a comic homage to the Four Marx Brothers), *Trader Hound* (a lampoon of the M-G-M African adventure *Trader Horn*) and *All Quiet on the Canine Front*. A posthumous Oscar, anyone?

Left: The always superb Madeline Kahn led an all-star cast that went nowhere fast in the lame 1976 comedy *Won Ton Ton: The Dog That Saved Hollywood,* though the film did attempt to recapture some sense of Rin Tin Tin's heyday. *Above and right:* Disney's 1959 *The Shaggy Dog* starred Fred MacMurray as a mailman who hates dogs—and whose son (Tommy Kirk) happens to be the victim of a curse that occasionally transforms him into an Old English sheepdog. The production values were strictly of television quality, and the movie today plays better in the memories of baby boomers than it does on home video.

Below: **Tom Hanks, as Detective Scott Turner, adopts a terminally drooling Dogue de Bordeaux in the odd-couple comedy *Turner & Hooch,* in which Hooch (here in bed with Turner) solves the murder of his previous master.**

Top left: The Ugly Dachshund was not a little sausage dog at all but a Great Dane who thinks he's a dachshund. Dean Jones and Suzanne Pleshette starred in the 1966 family film. Less charming than 1989's *Turner & Hooch* was the same year's *K-9 (left)* with Jim Belushi as a cop who enlists a shepherd (played by Jerry Lee) to help solve a drug case.

Hot Dogs: Or, Dogs in Heat

Walt Disney's irresistable *Lady and the Tramp* (1955) came from a short story by Ward Greene titled "Happy Dan, the Whistling Dog." Clearly, that wasn't meant to be Lady, a respectable cocker spaniel from a proper New England household. Her new acquaintance Tramp, from the other side of the tracks, easily could have been called Happy Dan, though in early script drafts that dated back to the 1940s, the male character was referred to as Homer, Rags, and even Bozo. Lady and the Bozo? Here, the two perfectly named lovers enjoy a plate of pasta that, thanks to one long single noodle, will soon lead to their first kiss.

Director Billy Wilder's 1948 *The Emperor Waltz,*
which Wilder cowrote with Charles Brackett,
contained some *Lady and the Tramp*–like
elements, in that its two protagonists hailed from
opposite ends of the socioeconomic spectrum.
Below: Bing Crosby and his dog Buttons
(here mimicking Nipper, the RCA trademark dog)
as two traveling gramophone salesmen working in
tandem in pre-World War II Austria. *Left:* Crosby's
love interest, Joan Fontaine, is Countess Johanna
von Stolzenberg-Stolzenberg. Her poodle is named
Sheherazade. By the end, the entire quartet ends
up happily mated. *Overleaf:* Missy and Beethoven,
two soulmates whose love is put to the test by an
alimony-seeking divorcée who dognaps Missy,
in the 1993 comedy *Beethoven's 2nd.*

Canine Cupids:
When Love Needs a Leg Up—or Four

Irene Dunne and Cary Grant played divorcing couple Lucy and Jerry Warriner in Leo McCary's 1937 classic screwball comedy *The Awful Truth.* At issue is who gets custody of Mr. Smith, played by Asta.

Cary Grant is driven to distraction, and to lady's garments, in Howard Hawks's 1938 breakneck screwball comedy *Bringing Up Baby*. That's the ubiquitous Asta (as George) looking on innocently as May Robson points an accusing finger.

Among the comic elements of 1945's *The Affairs of Susan*, starring Joan Fontaine, was this Great Dane suitably trained in the art of sniffing out a suitor.

Above: Janeane Garofalo played a mastiff-loving, Cyrano-like veterinarian/radio show hostess in 1996's delightful *The Truth About Cats & Dogs,* which, suffice it to say, exposed some truths about men and women.
Right: 1998's *Dog Park,* with Luke Wilson and Natasha Henstridge, failed to live up to its premise, which promised to show urban dog runs as the new singles bars.

Tom Hanks, who seems to play
opposite dogs as often as he
does Meg Ryan, online with his
golden retriever Brinkley in
Nora Ephron's cute but forced
You've Got Mail (1998).

Adam Sandler sure does remind me of Asta, right down to relieving his bladder. Come to think of it, Asta was more discreet. And just as naughty as his humans, Nick and Nora Charles. (Asta, that is.) Their excuse was that they liked to imbibe. Asta's excuse was that he did what pleased him. Didn't give a bone about what people thought. A dog's dog. —Coco

Camping with four Afghans: Dolores Gray as the seductress Lalume in M-G-M's silly 1955 adaptation of the musical *Kismet*, based on a Broadway show with music by Borodin and taken from the tales of the Arabian Nights. The hounds were nothing but props, but then, so was most of the cast.

Below: Steve Martin, fresh from the bathtub, makes do with what's at hand as he breathlessly pursues Bernadette Peters in 1979's *The Jerk*.

Left: Myrna Loy and William Powell as the most cosmopolitan of couples, Nick and Nora Charles (reputedly based upon the writers and lovers Lillian Hellman and Dashiell Hammett), and their surrogate child from *The Thin Man* series, Asta.

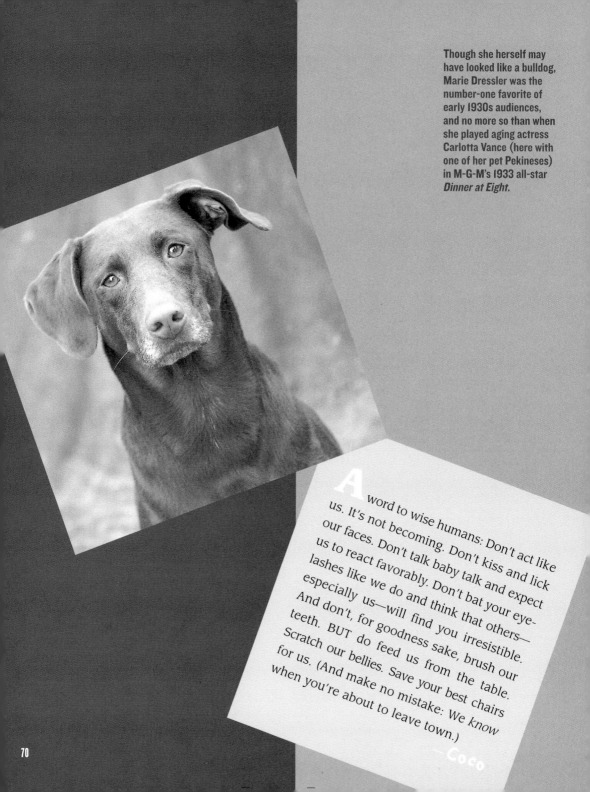

Though she herself may have looked like a bulldog, Marie Dressler was the number-one favorite of early 1930s audiences, and no more so than when she played aging actress Carlotta Vance (here with one of her pet Pekineses) in M-G-M's 1933 all-star *Dinner at Eight*.

A word to wise humans: Don't act like us. It's not becoming. Don't kiss and lick our faces. Don't talk baby talk and expect us to react favorably. Don't bat your eyelashes like we do and think that others—especially us—will find you irresistible. And don't, for goodness sake, brush our teeth. BUT do feed us from the table. Scratch our bellies. Save your best chairs for us. (And make no mistake: We *know* when you're about to leave town.)

~ *Coco*

Range Rovers: Pistol-Packin' Pooches

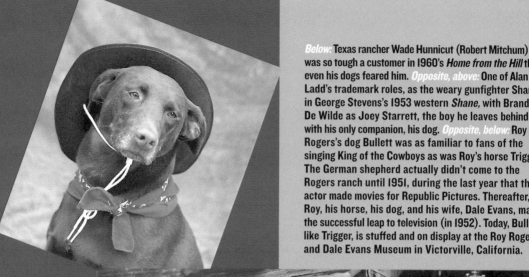

Below: Texas rancher Wade Hunnicut (Robert Mitchum) was so tough a customer in 1960's *Home from the Hill* that even his dogs feared him. *Opposite, above:* One of Alan Ladd's trademark roles, as the weary gunfighter Shane, in George Stevens's 1953 western *Shane,* with Brandon De Wilde as Joey Starrett, the boy he leaves behind—with his only companion, his dog. *Opposite, below:* Roy Rogers's dog Bullett was as familiar to fans of the singing King of the Cowboys as was Roy's horse Trigger. The German shepherd actually didn't come to the Rogers ranch until 1951, during the last year that the actor made movies for Republic Pictures. Thereafter, Roy, his horse, his dog, and his wife, Dale Evans, made the successful leap to television (in 1952). Today, Bullet, like Trigger, is stuffed and on display at the Roy Rogers and Dale Evans Museum in Victorville, California.

Family Friends:
The Unquestioned
Head of the
Household

Clockwise, from top left: The 1934 version of the poorhouse comedy *Mrs. Wiggs of the Cabbage Patch* starred W. C. Fields, ZaSu Pitts, and, as Klondike, this border terrier named Rex; another screen staple, the 1872 children's tale about a charcoal Bouvier called *A Dog of Flanders,* has been the subject of at least five movies, the first version made in 1914 (the one depicted here was released in 1935, and that's no Bouvier); the 1940 tearjerker *The Biscuit Easter* concerned a bird dog named Promise; Daisy the dog really ran the Bumstead household, which included Blondie, Dagwood, and Baby Dumpling Bumstead (Penny Singelton, Arthur Lake, and Larry Simms), gathered here for the original 1938 *Blondie.*

Above: **Monty Woolley as the irascible lodger Colonel Smollett, who over time strikes a peace with the bulldog Soda (who goes so well with whiskey), in David O. Selznick's 1944 wartime drama, *Since You Went Away*. With the two of them is Shirley Temple, who always got along with everyone.** *Right:* **Coco checks this week's grosses.**

Left: In Steven Spielberg's *E.T. The Extra Terrestrial,* the family mutt sensed before the others did that there was something in the house from three million light-years away. *Below:* Street tramp Jerry Baskin (Nick Nolte) loses his dog and decides to end his life in Paul Mazursky's 1986 *Down and Out in Beverly Hills,* but instead he ends up saving the rich and bored Whiteman family (whose members were played by Richard Dreyfuss, Bette Midler, and this border collie named Mike).

Above: Cruella De Vil's henchmen, Horace and Jasper Badun, don't see spots in front of their eyes as the puppies hide out in Walt Disney's 1961 *101 Dalmatians.*
Right: Daddy Dalmatian, Pongo, with a prize from wife Perdita's litter.
Opposite page: Jeff Daniels as Dalmatian owner Roger Radcliffe in the 1996 live-action remake of the animated favorite.
Overleaf: A veritable "Dalmatian plantation" from the 1996 feature. In 2000, there appeared a further adventure, *102 Dalmations,* featuring a kinder, gentler Cruella (Glenn Close).

When The Walt Disney Company made the live-action *101 Dalmatians,* a veritable Dalmatian deluge occurred. Humans demanded to have their own cute, real-life versions at home. But as the black-and-white pups grew up, their colorful Dalmatian dispositions came through. Even worse were the negative aspects of human nature that surfaced. Uncontrollable Dalmatians were suddenly abandoned en masse or else shoved into shelters. PLEASE be thoughtful. Don't adopt a pet you can't take care of and love. —Coco

Goody Four Paws:
Awwwww

No indigent waif is complete without a dog, even if it is a well-groomed wire-haired fox terrier (for once, not played by Asta), here with the quintessential waif, Janet Gaynor, in 1931's *Daddy Long Legs.*

Before having to contend with *The Shaggy Dog*, Fred MacMurray starred with this cairn terrier, as well as Claudette Colbert, in 1944's *Practically Yours*, a contrivance about a wartime pilot whose message to his dog is intercepted by a woman.

Clockwise, from top left: In 1951's *You Never Can Tell,* Peggy Dow serenades Rex, an ex-police dog who inherits an eccentric millionaire's fortune only to be murdered for his money (and then reincarnated as Dick Powell, who solves the killing); the 1961 *Greyfriars Bobby* recounted the Scottish tale of the faithful Skye terrier Bobby, who never leaves the side of his master, not even once the old man dies and is buried in Greyfriers Kirkyard; one of the running gags in 1960's *Please Don't Eat the Daisies,* starring Doris Day and David Niven, is how the family's city-raised sheepdog is scared of the suburbs. *Overleaf:* Benji on the run in the mid-1970s, before Sylvester Stallone thought to race through the streets in *Rocky.*

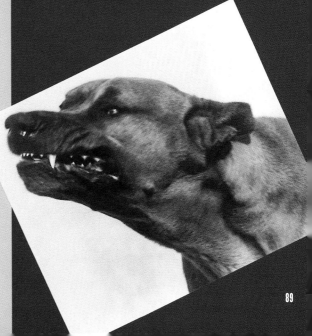

Opposite: In 1936's *Killer-Dog*, a ten-minute short, a mutt accused of murdering sheep is brought to trial. *Above:* As moody as his master, Heathcliff (Laurence Olivier), is the Great Dane of the house, in William Wyler's near-perfect 1939 interpretation of Emily Brönte's *Wuthering Heights. Right:* The very first Sherlock Holmes adventure to star Basil Rathbone as the super-sleuth was 1939's *The Hound of the Baskervilles*, a mystery about a trained killer who happens to have four legs.

Rabid bats turn a friendly St. Bernard named Cujo *(right)* into a monster from Hell *(far right)*, in the low-rent but memorable 1983 screen adaptation of the Stephen King novel, *Cujo.*

It's bad apples like Cujo who spoil the whole barrel for the rest of us. Though I once knew a Rottweiler who went out with the actor who played him. She wasn't impressed, if you catch my drift. Practically slept all through dinner. Plus, he snored.

—Coco

Loyal Companions: Those Who Love, Honor, and (Sometimes) Obey

Toto, the driving force behind Dorothy Gale's flight from Kansas, was the subject of the longest casting search having to do with M-G-M's triumphant 1939 *The Wizard of Oz*. Trainer Carl Spitz's cairn terrier, Terry, fit the look that the film's producers wanted, and Spitz was paid $125 a week for Terry's services. He could have held out for $500—the salary Judy Garland received.

In 1929, rising M-G-M star Clark Gable bought this police dog and named him Fels. Studio publicists also said that Gable (shown here with his buddy in 1932) trained the animal himself but that, unlike his master, Fels was not friendly. Funny how much Fels resembles Flash, M-G-M's dog of the 1920s.

In Cecil B. DeMille's 1927 epic *The King of Kings,* Christ (H. B. Warner) is crucified, then remembered by this faithful follower.

When a title tells all: from 1916's *A Man's Best Friend*,
directed by William Bertram.

Before Budweiser's Spuds Mackenize popularized bull terriers, Charles Dickens named a member of the breed Bull's Eye and provided him as a companion for the villainous Bill Sikes in *Oliver Twist*. *Above:* Robert Newton as Sikes in David Lean's 1947 version of the story. *Below:* Oliver Reed (accompanied by Mark Lester, as the Artful Dodger) in Carol Reed's sunnier 1968 musical version, *Oliver!*

In the Mississippi swamps, the orphaned Skeeter (Brandon DeWilde) and his Uncle Jesse (Walter Brennan) come to terms with one another thanks to the boy's pet basenji, in William Wellman's 1956 film *Goodbye, My Lady.*

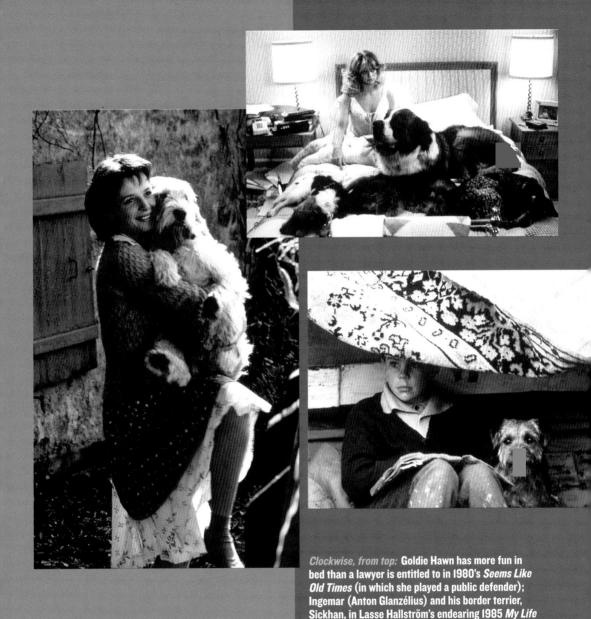

Opposite page, top to bottom: General George S. Patton's love for his bull terrier is such that he can even overlook the dog's lack of interest in the opposite sex (George C. Scott in 1970's *Patton*); Skip is prepared for his Army physical in *My Dog Skip* (2000).

Clockwise, from top: Goldie Hawn has more fun in bed than a lawyer is entitled to in 1980's *Seems Like Old Times* (in which she played a public defender); Ingemar (Anton Glanzélius) and his border terrier, Sickhan, in Lasse Hallström's endearing 1985 *My Life As a Dog*; Juliette Binoche in 1988's *The Unbearable Lightness of Being*, where the dog is as central to the love affair as Daniel Day-Lewis.

Above: One element that made 1995's *Babe* so winning, besides its sense of whimsy, was the very fact that the pig of the title thought he was a dog, thanks to the border collie who helped raise him. *Right:* The Castorini family of 1987's *Moonstruck,* in which one member's illicit affair is revealed to Grandpa one night while he's walking the dog. *Opposite page:* Ludwig Bemelmans's charismatic troublemaker Madeline was brought to life on the screen in 1998, with her dog Genevieve as part of the package.

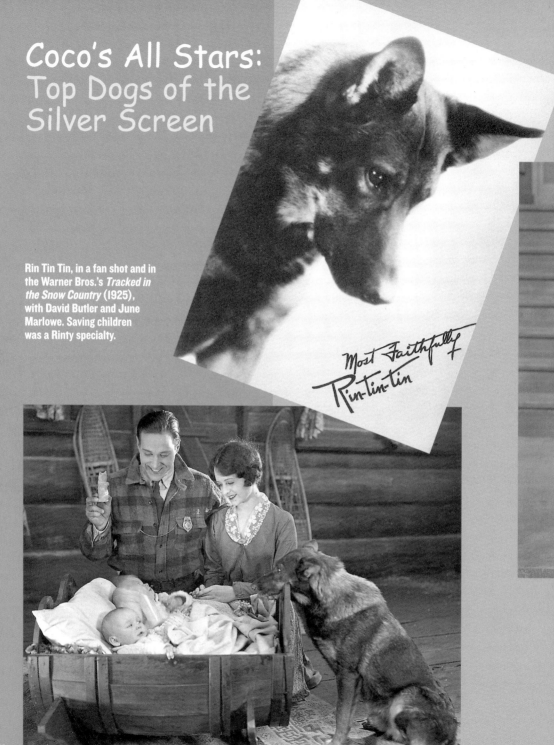

Coco's All Stars:
Top Dogs of the Silver Screen

Rin Tin Tin, in a fan shot and in the Warner Bros.'s *Tracked in the Snow Country* (1925), with David Butler and June Marlowe. Saving children was a Rinty specialty.

Most Faithfully
Rin-tin-tin

So widely accepted was Pete, or Petey, the pit bull of the Our Gang series (1922-42), that he was among the first of his kind to be registered as a Staffordshire bull terrier when, in 1935, the British Kennel Club began recognizing the breed. (The American Kennel Club refused to follow suit until nearly 40 years later, in 1974.) By the time the last delightful Gang escapade was filmed, at least a dozen dogs had played the photogenic pal with the trademark bull's eye.

Part of Pluto's appeal has always been that he never came across as a threat to anyone. Never bit. Never scratched. Never so much as chewed up a shoe. Let's face it, there wasn't a lot of brain power going on. Pluto's luckiest break? Having a lot of well-placed friends and a backer who understood merchandising. Slacker.
—Coco

Walt Disney's Pluto made his screen debut in the 1930 Mickey Mouse cartoon *The Chain Gang*, in which he was simply identified as a bloodhound. A year later, in *The Picnic*, he played Minnie's dog Rover. In 1933, Disney named him Pluto, a pet of Mickey's, in *The Moose Hunt*. And that's how he's remained.

Blondie started life as a rich 1930s playgirl in Chick Young's comic strip. She was domesticated by her husband, the former playboy Dagwood Bumstead, and their dog, a mutt named Daisy (as well as children Baby Dumpling and Cookie), and the strip emerged on screen starting in 1938, with Penny Singleton and Arthur Lake as the Bumsteads. Daisy's range included double takes (inspired by the comic actor Franklin Pangborn) and the perking up of her head whenever she was caught unaware. Alas, this latter trick was accomplished by a trainer tugging on thin, unseen wires attached to Daisy's ears. Pictured here is a scene from the 1940 *Blondie Plays Cupid*, with Larry Simms as Baby Dumpling.

Lassie? The Meryl Streep of dogdom. An untouchable, even when her part was taken by a male (her part in movies, that is). Able to hold her own against the young and flawless Elizabeth Taylor in her earliest movies, *both* their earliest movies. Lassie was one dog who should be envied. I mean, she had her very own table in the M-G-M commissary. No waiting for scraps. —Coco

The hound dog Sounder was as much a part of the Morgan family as any other member, in 1972's *Sounder,* which told of a group of Louisiana sharecroppers in 1933. Richard Roundtree headed the cast of the quiet, dramatic movie, which deserves a loud revival.

Matt Dillon holds Puffy, a border terrier who survives electrocution, an overdose of uppers, and a body cast in the tasteless but hilarious 1998 comedy *There's Something About Mary*. The dog served as one of the ways to the heart of the heroine, played charmingly by Cameron Diaz.

Acknowledgments

To those who not only helped with this book but who have, over time, proved to be good friends (and, sometimes, room-mates) to Coco, a mere thank-you is not enough. So, how about if I pass around my dog-eared copy of *Travels With Charley* to: Vernel Bagneris, Doug Becker, Stacey Behlmer, Richard Bernstein, Carol Carey, Mary Corliss, Bob Cosenza, Judith Crist, Evan Drutman, Estelle Ellis, Harry Haun, Chris Hill, Itay Hod, Jeff Holecko, Dolores Hope, Cynthia Johnson, Kevin Kurimsky, Peter McCrea, Howard Mandelbaum, Ron Mandelbaum, Dr. David Morowitz, Meredith Murray, Tim O'Shea, Ruth Peltason, Alex Pinsky, Gladys Poll, Anthony Portello, Vic Ramos, Diane Reid, David Robinson, Dorothy Sanson, Warren Schomaker, Pippa Scott, Joy Silverman, Miranda Tollman, Allison Trope, and Alice K. Turner.

Special thanks to the agent Martha Kaplan for her ingenuity in recognizing my infatuation with the then-recently acquired Coco and proposing this idea; to the book's brave, ultimate editor, Harriet Whelchel; to its exact ("What do you mean, no *Umberto D.*?") and imaginative designer, Carol Robson; to the clever cover artist, Joe Zeff; and to its indefatigable promoter (the book's fairy dogmother), Carol Morgan. And to Paul Gottlieb, of course, the publisher without whom Abrams just wouldn't be Abrams: Woof, woof.

—S.M.S.

The star of *My Dog Skip,* with Caitlin Wachs and Frankie Muniz, teaches his two human friends another important lesson in life: how to enjoy a movie. **THE END.**

Index of
Movies and Dogs

Dogs' names refer to character names (with the exception of Coco). Numbers refer to illustration pages.

Photograph Credits and Film Copyrights

The author and publisher wish to thank all of the institutions and organizations that provided photographs for the book:

The Kobal Collection: 9 below, 10, 14, 16, 21, 23, 27, 32 bottom, 34–35, 39 bottom, 41 top, 45, 46 top and bottom, 49, 52 top, 53 top and bottom, 54, 56 bottom, 57, 58–59, 60, 61, 65 top, 66 top, 67, 68, 73 top, 75 bottom, 78 top and bottom, 84 top, 88, 89 top (photograph by Coburn) and bottom, 90, 91, 92, 95, 96 top and bottom, 98 top and bottom, 99, 100 top, 101, 103, 105, 106 top, 107 top, 110–111. **Photofest:** endpaper, 25, 29, 30, 31 top, 32 top and middle, 33 left, 37 top right, 43, 47, 50–51, 55 top and bottom, 56 top, 62–63, 64, 66 bottom, 71, 73 bottom, 74 bottom , 75 top, 76 top, 77 top, 79 top, 80–81, 83, 84 bottom, 85, 94, 97, 100 bottom, 102 top and bottom, 104, 106 bottom, 107 bottom. **The Museum of Modern Art/Film Stills Archive:** 11, 13, 38, 44, 48, 69 top, 72 bottom, 74 top, 82, 93. **Courtesy of the Academy of Motion Picture Arts and Sciences:** 12

The Adventures of Milo and Otis © 1989 Columbia Pictures Industries, Inc. All Rights Reserved. Photograph by Greg Specht. *Air Bud: Golden Receiver* © Buddy Films, Inc. Photograph by Kharen Hill. *Air Bud* © Disney Enterprises, Inc. Photograph by Kharen Hill. *All Dogs Go To Heaven* © 1989 Goldcrest and Sullivan Bluth Limited. All Rights Reserved. Distributed by MGM Home Entertainment. *As Good As It Gets* © 1997 TriStar Pictures, Inc. All Rights Reserved. *Babe* © 1995 Universal City Studios, Inc. All Rights Reserved. Photograph by Carolyn Jones. *Balto* © 1995 Universal City Studios, Inc., and Amblin Entertainment, Inc. All Rights Reserved.

Beethoven © 1991 Universal City Studios, Inc. All Rights Reserved. Photograph by Christine Loss. *Beethoven's 2nd* © 1993 Universal City Studios, Inc. All Rights Reserved. *Best in Show* © Castle Rock Entertainment. Distributed by Warner Bros. *Cujo* © 1983 Sunn Classics Pictures, Inc. *Dr. Doolittle* © 1998 Twentieth Century Fox Film Corporation. *Dog Park* © 1999 New Line Productions, Inc. *Down and Out in Beverly Hills* © Touchstone Pictures. All Rights Reserved. *E.T. The Extra Terrestrial* © 1982 Universal City Studios, Inc. All Rights Reserved. *Greyfriars Bobby* © Disney Enterprises, Inc. *Homeward Bound: The Incredible Journey* © Disney Enterprises, Inc. *The Jerk* © 1979 Universal City Studios, Inc. All Rights Reserved. *K-9* © 1989 Universal Studios. All Rights Reserved. *Lady and the Tramp* © Disney Enterprises, Inc. Stills from *Lassie* courtesy of Paramount Pictures. *Madeline* © 1998 TriStar Pictures, Inc. All Rights Reserved. *Moonstruck* © 1987 Metro-Goldwyn-Mayer Studios Inc. All Rights Reserved. *My Life as a Dog* © Film Teknik/Svensk Filmindustri. Distributed by Skouras Pictures. *My Dog Skip* Photography © 2000 MDS Productions LLC., artwork © 2000 Warner Bros. Photographs by Jeanne Louise Bulliard. *Oliver & Company* © Disney Enterprises, Inc. *Old Yeller* © Disney Enterprises, Inc. *101 Dalmatians* © 1961 Disney Enterprises, Inc. *101 Dalmatians* © 1996 Disney Enterprises, Inc. *Pluto* cel © Disney Enterprises, Inc. *The Shaggy Dog* © Disney Enterprises, Inc. *The Truth About Cats & Dogs* © 1996 Twentieth Century Fox. Photograph by Merie W. Wallace. *There's Something About Mary* © 1998 Twentieth Century Fox Film Corporation. *Turner & Hooch* © Touchstone Pictures. All Rights Reserved. *The Ugly Dachshund* © Disney Enterprises, Inc. *The Unbearable Lightness of Being* © The Saul Zaentz company. Distributed by Orion Pictures Corporation. *White Fang* © Disney Enterprises, Inc. Photograph by Richard Foreman. *You've Got Mail* Program Content, Artwork, and Photography © 1998 Warner Bros.